Little PRESIDENT TRUMP'S NOTEBOOK

THE BLACK DIAMOND EFFECT® Volume 1, No. 38   —   LITTLE PRESIDENT TRUMP'S SANDBOX NOTEBOOK (PAPERBACK EDITION)
THE BLACK DIAMOND EFFECT® is a federal registered trademark of George Peter Gatsis. All prominent characters featured in the book and the distinctive likeness thereof are trademarks of George Peter Gatsis unless otherwise noted. "TBDE" is an abbreviation of THE BLACK DIAMOND EFFECT®.

LITTLE PRESIDENT TRUMP'S SANDBOX NOTEBOOK © 2024 George Peter Gatsis. All Rights Reserved.
Created, Book Design, Typesetting, Cover & Interior Art by George Peter Gatsis. © 2024 George Peter Gatsis. All Rights Reserved.

LITTLE PRESIDENT TRUMP'S SANDBOX NOTEBOOK © 2024 Critical Blast Publishing. All Rights Reserved.
Critical Blast Publishing, 24 Hillside Drive Suite A, Holiday Island, AR 72631

First Edition September 2024
0 9 8 7 6 5 4 3 2 1
ISBN: 978-1-998564-16-3   (PAPERBACK EDITION)